Weekend Fun

Let's Go to the
Museum

By Cate Foley

Welcome
Books

Children's Press
A Division of Scholastic Inc.
New York / Toronto / London / Auckland
Mexico City / New Delhi / Hong Kong
Danbury, Connecticut

Thanks to The Academy of Natural Sciences of Philadelphia, Philadelphia, PA

Photo Credits: Cover and all photos by Maura Boruchow
Contributing Editor: Jennifer Silate
Book Design: Michael DeLisio

Visit Children's Press on the Internet at:
http://publishing.grolier.com

Library of Congress Cataloging-in-Publication Data

Foley, Cate.
  Let's go to a museum / by Cate Foley.
    p. cm. -- (Weekend fun)
  Includes index.
  ISBN 0-516-23193-6 (lib. bdg.) -- ISBN 0-516-29583-7 (pbk.)
  1. Museums--Juvenile literature. 2. Museum exhibits--Juvenile literature. [1. Museums.]
  I. Title. II. Series.

AM7 .F65 2001
069'.5--dc21

                                                    2001017060

Contents

We are going to the **museum** today.

4

THE ACADEMY
OF
NATURAL SCIENCES
OF PHILADELPHIA

Mom buys tickets for our family to get into the museum.

6

There are many things to see at the museum.

We will see the **dinosaurs** first.

The museum has many dinosaur bones.

This is a dinosaur's head!

The museum has the teeth of animals, too.

This is a shark's tooth.

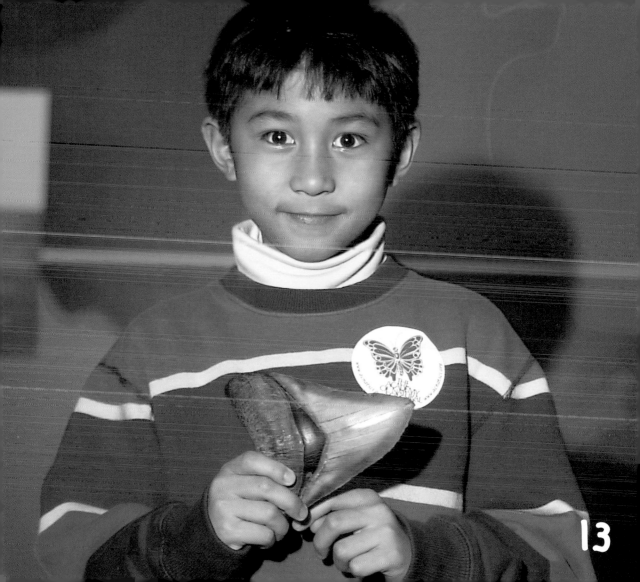

13

Next, we see the **butterflies**.

This butterfly is very big.

15

At the museum, there are also animals that we can pet.

I pet a rabbit.

It is very soft.

The museum also has
a **library**.

19

There are many books
in the library.

We read about
what we saw at the
museum today.

New Words

butterflies (**buht**-uhr-flyz) insects with slender bodies and wings, which are usually brightly colored

dinosaurs (**dy**-nuh-sorz) reptiles that lived millions of years ago

library (**ly**-brehr-ee) a room or building where books, magazines, and films are kept for public use

museum (myoo-**zee**-uhm) a building that displays a collection of objects of art, science, or history

To Find Out More

Books
The Museum
by Stuart A. Kallen
Abdo Publishing Company

Visiting the Art Museum
by Laurene Krasny Brown
NAL Dutton

Web Site
San Diego Natural History Museum Kid's Habitat
http://www.sdnhm.org/kids/dinosaur/index.html
On this site, you can play a word search game and
learn facts about dinosaurs.

Index

About the Author
Cate Foley writes and edits books for children. She lives in New Jersey with her husband and son.

Reading Consultants
Kris Flynn, Coordinator, Small School District Literacy, The San Diego County Office of Education

Shelly Forys, Certified Reading Recovery Specialist, W.J. Zahnow Elementary School, Waterloo, IL

Sue McAdams, Former President of the North Texas Reading Council of the IRA, and Early Literacy Consultant, Dallas, TX